Performing Feminism:

Self/maintenance in contemporary art and society

Dana Leslie

An imprint of Boom Publications Ltd

272 Bath Street
Glasgow SCOTLAND
G2 4JR

Boom Graduates and the logo are trademarks of Boom Publications Ltd.

Boom Publications Ltd is a more-than-profit company, dedicating over half our profits to university scholarships for underprivileged students worldwide. In order to offset our carbon footprint, we also pledge to plant a tree for each graduation book commissioned.

Performing Feminism: Self/Maintenance in Contemporary Art and Society
was first published in Great Britain in 2022.

Copyright © Dana Leslie. Dana Leslie has asserted her right under the
Copyright, Designs and Patents Act, 1988,
to be identified as Author of this work.
For legal purposes any Acknowledgements constitute
an extension of this copyright page.
Cover design by Boom Graduates Ltd and the Book Cover Zone USA.

All rights are reserved. No part of this publication may be reproduced or transmitted in any form or by any means, electronic or mechanical, including photocopying, recording, or any information storage or retrieval system, without prior permission in writing from the publishers.

Boom Publications Ltd do not have any control over, or responsibility for any third-party websites referred to or in this book. All internet addresses given in this book were correct at the time of going to press. The author and publisher regret any inconvenience if addresses have changed or sites have ceased to exist, but can accept no responsibility for any such changes.

Typeset by Helen at Boom Graduates.
Printed and bound in the UK.

To find out more about our authors and books visit www.boomgraduates.com
and sign up for our newsletters.

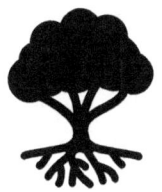

We plant a tree for every
Boom Graduate book commissioned, and
thereafter plant a tree for every 10 books sold.

THG
(more : trees)

MEMBER

Watch our forest grow at
https://moretrees.eco/forest/BoomPublicationsLtd/

Dana Leslie

Performing Feminism:

Self/Maintenance in Contemporary Art and Society

Dana Leslie

Performing Feminism

"One is not born, but rather becomes, a woman"

Simone de Beauvoir

"We as woman have a right to ask, 'What is art? What do we want it to be?' and see our answers validated."

Judy Chicago

Dana Leslie

Contents

Author biography 11

Abstract 13

Introduction 15

Chapter one 21

The Full-Time, Unpaid Role of a Woman: Mother, Wife, Cook, Cleaner 21

Chapter 2 37

Becoming a Manmade Woman: 37

Goodbye Housework 37

Chapter 3 53

Cash, Commodity and Commercialisation: 53

The unreasonable importance of self-maintenance for women in contemporary society and the art world today ... 53

Conclusion 67

References 71

Glossary 85

Glossary reference list 97

Further Reading 103

Acknowledgements 107

BOOM! 109
A note about Boom Graduates 111
Notes... 115

Author biography

Dana Leslie is a multidisciplinary artist and feminist based in Dundee, Scotland. Her practice encompasses moving-image, installation, photography, print-making, writing, and performance. She often tackles political and feminist themes in her work, encouraging interaction, engagement, and revaluation. Dana aims to intertwine the personal and impersonal and eradicate the distance we put between ourselves and the stories we read. Most recently, she has created a digital theatre piece funded by Creative Scotland for False Start Productions, showcased her undergraduate Degree Show at Duncan of Jordanstone College of Art and Design, and has been selected to participate in Scotland and Venice's Professional Development Programme 2022. Dana was a recipient of the 2022 InGEAR Publishing Awards at the University of Dundee.

Dana Leslie

Abstract

In Simone de Beauvoir's *The Second Sex* (1949) it is argued that women are defined by the society they live in, culturally mirroring patriarchal expectations. Throughout the late 1960s and 1970s the second wave of feminism impacted the contemporary artworld. Many female artists turned to performance art to explore and critique the gender role prescribed to women as 'housewife'. Mierle Laderman Ukeles, tired of having to separate her motherly duties from her artistic practice, wrote *Manifesto for Maintenance Art 1969!*. Through combining her labour and art, Ukeles intersected life and performance. As feminists achieved more equal opportunities, and women were no longer secluded in the domestic field, beauty work became a new form of oppression. Lynn Hershman Leeson further blurred the boundary between art, performance and female identity during this period through creating a fictitious persona, *Roberta Breitmore* (1974-1978). Breitmore slipped into modern day society, gathering bureaucratic documents manifesting her into existence. These first instances of performance art as durational, maintenance-led, surveillance filled constructions reflecting real life for women at this time, can be compared with more recent expectations for females to perform and express themselves in adherence to the male gaze. The benefit of beauty work is publicity. The once unorthodox notion of 'playing a version of yourself' has become a way of life due to the historical and contemporary narratives that have been written for women, which feminist artists have exploited for their own artistic expression.

Introduction

In the 1970s there was social rebellion in the Western World. Texts such as Betty Friedan's *The Feminine Mystique* (1963) and Simone de Beauvoir's *The Second Sex* (1949) gained popularity and promoted feminist discourse. Women began to enter the political sphere and second-wave feminism emerged. The activism spread into many female artists' work, inspiring them to merge their life and art practice as a form of critique, and as what Beauvoir defined as 'woman as the other'. Beauvoir (1949, p.293) believed that man had made himself the focus of society and had prescribed roles to women that were beneficial to him: 'One is not born, but rather becomes, a woman'.

Beauvoir comments on gender as opposed to genetically predetermined sex, inferring a woman's identity is fabricated by the society she lives in, and forced to comply with ideals. In order to expose the daily discrimination women faced due to social oppression, many artists turned to performance art as a tool of expression. Feminist art historian and critic, Moira Roth, analyses the choice of medium in context of the political upheaval:

> The 1970s was an amazing decade for women…in pursuit of the goal of equal rights, women scrutinised and restructured their private and public lives. [Art] served both to mirror and to comment on these profound social, cultural and psychological changes. By 1970 women artists had discovered that performance art – a hybrid form which combines visual arts, theatre, dance, music, poetry and ritual – could be a particularly suitable form in which to explore their reassessments of themselves (Jacob and Roth, 1983, p.8).

The Women's Liberation Movement sought to achieve equal-pay and allow more women to move out of domesticity, hoping to eradicate the myth of man as breadwinner, and woman as housewife. Men were at an advantage career-wise as they did not have to split into the roles that fall under homemaker (mother, wife, cook, cleaner); maintenance work that was the unpaid woman's job. The artist Mierle Laderman Ukeles confronted this unfair system of oppression in her work by framing her household chores as artworks, and performing them in art institutions. Through her art Ukeles made the invisible visible.

After women successfully accessed the workforce, time-consuming beauty work took over from time-consuming housework; self-maintenance became the new system of gender oppression. Women had to adhere to impossible beauty standards to feel tolerated and increase their self-esteem. In Germaine Greer's ground-breaking book, *The Female Eunuch* (1986, p.76) Greer states 'it is agreed that "girls take more bringing up" than boys: what that really means is that girls must be more relentlessly supervised and repressed if the desired result is to ensue'. Lynn Hershman Leeson invented a persona who, through living in a patriarchal society, was oppressed and became an authentic woman reflecting the reality of female identity.

The benefit of women conforming to cultural beauty myths is publicity. To be beautiful is to be seen, and to be seen is to be consumed. Images of young, hyper-sexualised women sell. Women are objectified in the male-dominated media creating ideologies; a woman can no longer be separated from her appearance. Scrutinised, her value is attached to her body rather than talent or intellect. Tracey Emin's autobiographical work which examines female identity can be used as a case study on how self-maintenance affects a woman's success in the artworld, presented alongside similar contemporary examples across several industries.

Through the use of their art and body therefore, female artists have fought to subvert the injustices women face that keep them at a disadvantage compared to their male counterparts, exploiting conventional myths for their own artistic and personal development, inciting a cultural shift.

This book is formed of three chapters: Chapter 1. 'The Full-Time, Unpaid Role of a Woman: Mother, Wife, Cook, Cleaner'; Chapter 2. 'Becoming a Manmade Woman:

Goodbye Housework, Hello Beauty Work'; and Chapter 3. 'Cash, Commodity and Commercialisation: The unreasonable importance of self-maintenance for women in contemporary society and the art world today'. The book also contains a useful resource list following the conclusion which it is hoped the reader will find useful.

Dana Leslie

Chapter one

The Full-Time, Unpaid Role of a Woman: Mother, Wife, Cook, Cleaner

In 1971, art historian Linda Nochlin published her essay *Why Have There Been No Great Women Artists?* dissecting the theory of the gendered "genius", analysing why male artists were perceived to be innately talented and consequently more successful. Nochlin critiqued the circumstances in which artists produce their art, highlighting the unfair disparities between the sexes' working conditions, and the cultural exclusion of women throughout history:

> Things as they are and as they have been, in the arts as in a hundred other areas, are stultifying, oppressive, and discouraging to all those,

women among them, who did not have the good fortune to be born white, preferably middle class, and, above all, male (Nochlin, 2021, p.150).

Nochlin rejects the argument of male aptitude as biological, and instead reasons women have been neglected and conditioned to inferiority through lack of education at the hands of men (Nochlin, 2021). This can be seen as a fact when compared to other civilisations, such as the Ashanti women of the ethnic group Akan, which is a matrilineal society emphasising female leaders (Hernadon, 1991).

Philosopher Jean-Jacques Rousseau (1762, p.328) believed women's education 'ought to be relative to mens'; as he observed society withholding a woman's cultivation so they would perform mindless, menial tasks encouraging restraint and docility. He writes, 'women [should be] uniformly employed in a variety of duties, so that one talent should not be encouraged at the expense of others' (Rousseau, 1762, p.331). Although not written in the context of pursuing artistic endeavours, his statement can be applied to all elements of a women's life that is not serving a man; whether it is becoming a master of the arts or devoting herself to another career, it is not to be done in place of being a dutiful wife, homemaker and mother. This trope has remained prevalent; in *The Physiology of Marriage*, the male author declares '[wives] must be denied training and culture, forbidden to develop their individuality' (Balzac, 1829). Dr Gregory takes this one step further writing:

> The intention of your being taught needle-work [and] knitting…is not on account of the intrinsic value of all you can do with your hands, which is trifling, but…enable you to fill up, in a tolerably agreeable way, some of the many solitary hours you must necessarily pass at home (Gregory, 1808, p.52).

Even when learning a skill, for women the purpose is to remain mindlessly occupied as to not engage in any unwarranted, non-beneficial activities, such as becoming an artist. Nochlin summarises the term "lady-painter" to mean 'a modest, proficient, self-demeaning level of amateurism' (Nochlin, 2021, p.164). An image of a 1933 news article recently went viral which read 'Wife of the Master Mural Painter Gleefully Dabbles in Works of Art' (Davies, 1933). The wife-artist was none other than Frida Kahlo. Even as recently as 2017, the artist Kate Miller was reduced to the contradicting headline 'T. J. Miller's wife making a name for herself in New York' (since edited to actually include her first name) (Bates, 2018; Siegler, 2017).

Mierle Laderman Ukeles sought to simultaneously expose the under-appreciated role of the woman and inequality in the artworld, and wrote *Manifesto for Maintenance Art 1969!*. The text was in direct response to Ukeles' lack of time to devote to her art practice. She believed female artists were at a disadvantage compared to their male-counterparts solely because they were women. Ukeles, frustrated with the burden of her domestic duties, reframed her art practice declaring 'Everything I say is Art is Art. Everything I do is Art is Art' (Harrison and Wood, 2003, p.918). The artist's new outlook resulted in her creating a series of artworks in the early 1970s in which she would scrub the floor of a museum's outside stairway and entrance. The performance criticised how undervalued maintenance work was, many viewers most likely presuming that Ukeles was a cleaner rather than an artist, and would not stop to watch. As stated by Parker & Pollock: 'The reality of housework is as invisible as the woman artist' (1987, p.139).

The patriarchy invented the myth that women should stay restricted in the private sphere as homemaker, and men should be in the working environment as the breadwinner: 'The world would be upside down if the woman went out to work and the husband stayed home to care for the house and children!' (Bott, 1957, p.197). Feudalism required everyone to be a worker in the home. The introduction of a capitalist society alongside industrialisation created a sexual division of labour (Gimenez, 2005): 'Work came to be defined as labour power which could be sold for a wage which, in turn, could buy other commodities' (Fransella and Frost, 1977). As women were treated as baby-making machines, the men went to work and left women to do any 'house' work in service to help the 'real' worker in the family. Sweeney disputes the wearisome duties of a homemaker are more than just washing and babysitting and believed that these routine actions 'produce' and 'reproduce' other workers (Parker and Pollock, 1987). Ukeles, recognising this imbalance, states maintenance work 'keeps the dust off the pure individual creation' in her manifesto (Harrison and Wood, 2003, p.918). Ukeles argues that women, by carrying the burden of all the unpaid domestic tasks, allow men the time and freedom to keep creating and working in order for society to function as it has. Whilst women are forced to split themselves into numerous roles: mother, wife, cook, cleaner; men can further their career.

Housework is an overlooked labour as it can never be judged as 'complete'. The goal is not to temporarily have clean clothes, a tidy house, a fed baby and a cooked meal, but rather to continuously achieve all of these things all of the time; it is cyclical. Never-ending work does not produce a commodity to sell at the end of the day. In essence, the labour of housework is only realised when the maintaining of the standard drops. As Parker and Pollock declare 'a women's work is never done' (Parker and Pollock, 1987, p.139).

In 1970 it was estimated that women spent on average seventy hours a week on their domestic duties (Oakley, 1974). *Penn World Table* reports the average annual working hours of an employee in 1970 was 1,871, roughly 36 hours per week. If women were paid equally for maintaining the house, they would have earned nearly double that of their male counterpart. In other words, in every home, women were performing the necessary, repetitive tasks, much like the monotonous factory work the men undertook daily, but women were doing this for free. Greer summarises the fate of the female homeworker as 'the housewife is an unpaid worker in her husband's house in return for the security of being a permanent employee' (Greer, 1986, p.242). Without being able to sell their labour, women were unable to save money, control their finances and even, sadly, leave their husbands if they so wished.

Economist Marilyn Waring acknowledges that all men benefit from this power dynamic and therefore won't willingly forsake it (Roberts, 1989). Men can continue rising to the top of the workforce, controlling who is hired and fairly compensated, whilst women maintain this system by eradicating all chores from the man's life - including raising the next generation of workers. Men can dedicate themselves to being an artist, or any job, without having to lose hours in another area of their life. Men can create; women must maintain.

Sweeney, in *Strategy for Women's Liberation* (1977), distinguishes 'that housework is unwaged means first of all that it appears not as work, but as part of our female nature' (Parker and Pollock, 1987, p.104). When writer Laura Bates visited a primary school and asked the children what activities were for girls, she declared that her heart sank when they responded with activities such as cleaning and cooking, whereas sports and science were the options the boys chose (Bates, 2018). In *Women, Art and the Power of Looking* the author writes that women are made to 'promote an idea of "home" as a stage-set on which an ideological version of family life and feminine virtue is performed' (McCormack, 2021, p.113). Sex-role norms are not biological, rather they have been manifested and prescribed by men throughout history - whether by mandate to ensure women stayed secluded in the Gynaeceum in ancient Greece, or instilling that the woman-worker is heavily desired during wartime – thus, the role of a woman bends around the wants and systematic needs of a society ruled by men.

Tavris (1973) found that when given two lists, one with traits typically seen as 'feminine' the other 'masculine' - such as nurturance for women and aggression for men - roughly three-quarters of people stated the differences were biological rather than cultural. Such thinking is easily refuted, the female identity at birth as carer is no more innate and set in stone than a male baby being a professional footballer – it takes years of practice, encouragement and institutionalised attitudes to confirm such behaviour as, and is acceptable. The only responsibility within the term 'homemaker' that a male is naturally prohibited from fulfilling is childbirth (Fransella and Frost, 1977). The housewife could just as easily be the househusband, but society has not yet taught or accepted this outlook.

Greer evidences 'the few men who do a hand's turn around the house expect gratitude and recognition, so sure are they that, though it is their dirt, it is not their job' (Greer, 2007, p.169). Feminist artist, Judy Chicago shares her experience in her memoir *Through the Flower: My Struggle as a Woman Artist*, recalling an early encounter she had with her husband aptly writing 'What makes you think that by biological accident, I was born with a cunt, I am supposed to pick up your socks?' (Chicago, 1982, p.22).

For Marx, the purpose of ideology is to present the beliefs of the ruling class as fact, an individual's concept of 'self' is socially determined and not a natural attribute (Fiske, 1990). The media not only reaffirms gender roles but shapes them, coercing society to act in accordance with their male-established standards. Advertisements form stereotypes by repetitively presenting the same habitual image of a person and their customary surroundings (Correa, 2009). Flooded with imagery, individuals create media-influenced narratives that directly influence their consciousness of who they are (Gauntlett, 2002). Ideals and values are placed onto these images, the adverts becoming a form of social reinforcement (Roy, 1998). According to a 1972 *Journal of Broadcasting* study, three-quarters of all advertisements featuring women were for bathroom or kitchen items (Dominick and Rauch, 1972). Women were also significantly less likely to be shown in a career setting or even outside of the home, but twice as likely to be with children. These images mould society's opinion of what a woman is and where she belongs, establishing falsehoods that can quickly spread as cultural norms and reinforce myths such as woman as housewife, husband as breadwinner.

In 1971 a study investigated 'women who perform the social role of housewife'. Lopata (1971) questioned *what are the most important roles of a woman, in order?*. The results demonstrate how housewives and working women prioritise responsibilities in line with typical societal expectations. When both groups ranked in order of importance the top three were close: mother (74%), wife (71%), housewife (58%), whereas duty towards self (8%) and friend/neighbour (4%) were significantly less-valued (Lopata, 1971).

Betty Friedan, having worked in the magazine industry, grew tired of perpetuating these glamorised depictions of domestic life in her job, and left intending to expose a generation of women's dissatisfaction with their lack of identity and prospects (Gauntlett, 2002). Her book *The Feminine Mystique* is widely agreed to have initiated the second-wave of feminism.

'The 1950s assumed that women would work until the birth of their first child' (Tuchman, 1978), it was widely believed. Ukeles was sceptical of marrying her husband as it was assumed women would remain at home once married (Finkelpearl, 2001). One art tutor expressed his sorrow when learning she was pregnant, assuming she would immediately forsake her art practice. Frustrated at his presumption Ukeles voiced:

> People only saw me as a mother. The culture had no place for me. There were no words for my life. I was split into two people: artist and mother. I had fallen out of the picture. I was in a fury. (Liss, 2009, p.52).

Ukeles is not alone; Mary Kelly infamously included her baby's dirty nappies in her installation *Post-Partum Document* (1973-1979). Kelly stated she 'wasn't trying to be revolutionary' but simply the nappies were 'the evidence' of the work she was doing (Eriksson, 2010). Like Ukeles, Kelly brought the private, secluded life of mothers into the spotlight, showcasing not merely a representation of all the menial, undervalued work women do, but an artefact preserving the state of existence before intervention. Furthermore, many female artists have spoken out regarding the detriment intimate heteronormative relationships and the chores of subsequent motherhood have on their careers, with many opting not to entertain the option at all.

> By becoming fully myself creatively...I put myself outside the structure of most female/male relationships...As difficult as this situation...is for me, the opportunity to work to my full potential has been worth the emotional deprivation and pain. (Chicago, 1982, p.214).

Woman cannot devote herself entirely to the duties of mother or career whilst there is temptation of the other (Beauvoir, 1949). Tracey Emin agrees 'there are good artists that have children. Of course there are. They are called men' (Groskop, 2015), confessing she could either be 100% mother or artist, but could not compromise. Revealing there is always a cost of a woman's choice, one will simply lose personal fulfilment or family life.

The effects of the gender division of labour are still relevant today, propelled by the Coronavirus pandemic. As many are still working from home and school closures are ongoing, a third of mothers are losing working hours due to constraints of childcare, with disabled mothers being the worst affected, followed by BAME women, then white women - with white men least affected (Fawcett Society, 2020; 2021). Pre-pandemic, *Mumsnet* (2019) conducted a survey which suggests that the myth of the male breadwinner is evident today: 96% of the website's users stated that the impact of having children affected women's careers negatively, compared to only 9% for men, and three-quarters agree that mothers would be higher ranking in the workforce had they not had children.

MP Rachel Reeves, on planning to continue working whilst pregnant, suffered backlash from fellow MP Andrew Rosindell who questioned her commitment to political duties claiming 'people need to be put in the positions they can handle' (Perraudin, 2015). Maternity discrimination is still rife today with the Equality and Human Rights Commission revealing that one in eight women lose their job due to pregnancy (Adams et al, 2016). However, this is of course all bound up with the "man-madeness" of women. In the 1950s, women were expected to be the perfect housewife – arguably today, despite being in the workplace, women are often still expected to be the perfect housewife. However, today they are also expected to do beauty work (on themselves) as well as housework, as well as often working full-time. The next chapter, 'Becoming a nmade Woman: goodbye housework, hello beauty work' will now explore this in more detail.

Chapter 2

Becoming a Manmade Woman: Goodbye Housework

During the second-wave of feminism as women became more political - succeeding in gaining the Equal Pay Act 1970 and achieving reproductive rights - a new form of oppression was growing in place of domesticity. With increasing numbers of women entering the workforce, creating higher competition for men, capitalist society needed an ideal for women to devote time to and invest money in. Naomi Wolf titled this new system of exploitation *The Beauty Myth* (Wolf, 1991) explaining 'inexhaustible but ephemeral beauty work took over from inexhaustible but ephemeral housework' (Wolf, 1991, p.16).

The myth was not entirely a new concept – affluent Victorian women risked their lives ingesting tapeworm eggs, hoping they would grow to eat excess fat (Zapata, 2016) – but it became the primary system of oppression. Women suddenly had to juggle homelife, a career and upkeeping their public image to reap the benefits afforded to compliant women in this new societal hierarchy. Greer states 'a good deal of the unpaid work younger women do is maintenance of a hairless, odourless, band-box self' (Greer, 2007, p.155). For women entering work, extreme fitness regimes, dieting, makeup routines and haircare replaced the time technological advancements in household appliances had freed up.

In his seminal text, *Ways of Seeing*, John Berger (1972) claims women must constantly observe themselves in relation to men, as men hold the power to define their successes. He states '[women's] own sense of being in herself is supplanted by a sense of being appreciated by another'. He continues, 'she is almost continually accompanied by her own image of herself…she comes to consider the surveyor and the surveyed within her as the two constituent yet always distinct elements of her identity as a woman' (Berger, 1972, p.46).

Berger suggests that a woman looks through the male gaze when viewing herself, consequently separating herself into the masculine viewer and the viewed object, eradicating her true self in the process. Radical feminist Shulamith Firestone agrees, suggesting the beauty ideal has transposed from originally meaning to appear beautiful to having an 'inanimate' perspective (Firestone, 1979, p.147). Singer Dolly Parton has stated that she sees herself simultaneously as puppet and puppet-master when discussing her persona and appearance (Hari, 2012). Greer declares, 'For she is a doll: weeping, pouting or smiling, running or reclining, she is a doll' (Greer, 1986, p.60). Rousseau (1762) observed that little girls adore dolls because they are, of course, destined to become one.

> Living a doll's life seems to have become an aspiration for many young women, as they leave childhood behind only to embark on a project

of grooming, dieting and shopping that aims to achieve the bleached, waxed, tinted look of a Bratz or Barbie doll (Walter, 2010, p.2)

Laura Bates describes the *Monster High* dolls' website, stating that one doll's hobbies were listed as 'shopping and flirting with boys', further declaring 'plucking and shaving is definitely a full-time job' (Bates, 2018).

Moreover, a version of Barbie was sold, which despite having a limited verbal repertoire, would announce 'Math class is tough', followed by babysitter-Barbie which included a book titled *How to Lose Weight* which gave the disturbing instruction 'don't eat' to her young, impressionable buyers (Lacey, 2012). With three Barbies reportedly selling every second (Christie's, 2006), Barbie's advice implying a girl should focus on her looks and not her studies, has a big reach: 'The further from the natural a female form, the more attractive it becomes. The further from the natural a female form, the more feminine it is' (Greer, 2007, p31). This observation explains why in 2015 the cosmetic surgery market in the US was valued at $20 billion (Archard et al,

2017). As Dolly Parton states 'It costs a lot to look this cheap' (Hari, 2012). 'Cosmetic surgery processes the bodies of woman-made women, who make up the vast majority of its patient pool, into man-made women' (Wolf, 1991, p.220). The man-made woman now outside of the home, must not see herself as a person but an aesthetic object whose only purpose is to costly deform themselves rather than pursue aspirations.

The women-made man however, does not exist - not even figuratively. Feminist artist Margaret Harrison's solo show was closed-down in 1971 by police on the grounds of 'obscenity' and 'indecency' (Rebel Women: The Great Art Fight Back, 2018). The policemen were insulted by the drawings of famous men, such as Hugh Hefner and Captain America, dressed as pin-up women donning high-heels and suspenders whilst revealing their large-illusory breasts. Yet when male artist Allen Jones exhibited *Hatstand, Chair and Table* (1969), in which he depicts scantily-clad women as furniture, he was branded an international sensation (Sladen, 1995).

This highlights the deep-rooted institutionalised sexism women face in life and art. The further away men are from the over-exaggerated feminine form, the more masculine they are perceived to be, therefore the less self-maintenance they have to do.

Wolf writes, '[the myth] is always actually prescribing behaviour and not appearance' (Wolf, 1991, p.14). Berger's and Wolf's theories correlate with Simone de Beauvoir's analysis that being born female is not the same as being a woman, but rather a constructed gender identity through social conditioning. Judith Butler (1988) encapsulates gender as 'identity instituted through a stylised repetition of acts', acts indeed such as beauty work. Drag queen RuPaul once professed 'you're born naked, and the rest is drag' (Keeps, 1993), implying that anything imposed onto one's body after birth is a performance of gender expression. The etymology of the word drag may have derived from 'grand rag', an archaic phrase for a masquerade ball where one would mask one's true identity (Joseph, 2021).

In the 1970s the artist Lynn Hershman Leeson undertook a durational performance which questioned the concept of self and blurred the line between fact and fiction. Feminist scholar, Peggy Phelan, writes of the legacy of Roberta Breitmore as 'a feminist critique of the psychic costs of femininity as masquerade' (Leeson and Weibel, 2016, p.106). *The Roberta Breitmore Series* (1973-1978) saw Hershman Leeson transform not just her appearance but into 'a fully-fledged, "complete" personality who existed over an extended period of time and whose existence could be proven in the world through physical evidence' (Gregos, 2011). Hershman Leeson defines Roberta Breitmore as an allegory, a representation of all women in contemporary society (Hershman Leeson, 1996). The artist may have created Breitmore from nothing, but through living in 1970s America, Breitmore became a person with real experiences who reflected the culture of this time for single women. Breitmore went on a series of unsuccessful dates; unable to find a man, she described herself as lonely in her diary (Walker Art Centre, 1977). Through multiple studies,

Carlson (1970) found that 'women define themselves by their relationships with other people' whereas men do not self-evaluate based on interpersonal relations (Carlson, 1970, p.265). Gregos states that Breitmore was sexually harassed and in true danger. Indeed, rape and women's safety was a big concern in 1970's California, and subsequently Breitmore visited a psychiatrist (Gregos, 2011). The psychiatric evaluation notes that Breitmore's issues stem from difficulty finding a job and losing weight (Walker Art Centre, 1978). Breitmore joined weightwatchers – which despite only being founded in 1963, was already a multi-million-dollar company – hoping to alleviate her consequent depression. The encounters Roberta had directly impacted the formation of her identity. Throughout the psychiatric session, surveillance photos of Breitmore were taken which Hershman Leeson used to produce *Roberta's Body Language Chart* (1978). The chart analyses Roberta's mannerisms in the context of female stereotypes. Text beside each photograph questions whether the artist's posture appears frigid or uptight, detaching her internal-self from her external-self, surveying her body how others may determine it. Breitmore's despair at her failure to lose weight and secure a man, reinforces Berger's ideology that success for women is relative to men's view of their worth. Roberta Breitmore was not born a woman but became a woman by being a victim of cultural determinism.

The Institute of Personal Care Science of Australia calculated that the global cosmetic industry in 2015 was worth US$334 billion (Ramli, 2015). Greer connects the pressure for women to look good and portray well in order to feel good:

> A man who is slovenly and untidy is considered normal; the woman who is either is a slut or a slommack…a woman who is dirty is dirt. The external attribute becomes a moral quality, as it does not for a man (Greer, 2007, p.171).

A study found that on average, adult women spend 55 minutes daily maintaining their appearance, totalling 335 hours per year (Today/AOL, 2014). Combined with the average one-hour-a-day of housework (established in chapter one), women are at a loss of 700 hours a year compared to men – nearly an entire month spent on maintenance and self-maintenance. When split into the average forty-hour working week, this equates to over a third of the working calendar. Furthermore, over two-thirds of women confirm makeup is a daily obligation; with roughly a third stating they would 'never leave the house' without it (Today/AOL, 2014, p.4). The report discloses that women invest this much time because they want to feel 'better about themselves' (Today/AOL, 2014).

Roberta Breitmore becomes a woman through attempting to adhere to beauty standards, and her face is constructed through the use of cosmetics and artifice. In *Roberta's Construction Chart 1*, her face is split into sections. A diagram drawn over the portrait shows which materials are needed to manipulate Leeson into Breitmore. Some of the essential, expensive branded products listed are: *Dior eyestick light*, *Revlon "Peach Blush"* and *"Date Mate" scarlet lipstick*. The chart closely resembles a paint-by-numbers activity, helpfully providing a step-by-step guide for women everywhere on how to paint a pre-approved stereotypical pretty face - anybody can become Roberta if they buy the products. The artist arranged for several other women to become Breitmore simultaneously, using the chart to create multiples of her persona (Leeson and Weibel, 2016).

Roberta's construction can be likened with contemporary society's complex beauty regimes, with women hoping to imitate the new, fashionable face endorsed by cosmetic brands. Contouring gives a person the ability to redesign their facial features. In *Medical Makeup for Concealing Facial Scars,* the authors compare contouring to sculpting with clay:

> Envision how you wish to reshape a feature; anywhere you would push or sculpt off clay would need a darker colour (contour) and

> anywhere you would add clay would need a light colour (highlight) (Mee and Wong, 2012, p.540).

Women are reshaping and maintaining their masks daily, a time-consuming and expensive endeavour. Regardless of busy schedules, work routines or ageing, this is a skill women are required to master without complaint. When beauty-empire owner Kylie Jenner was photographed barefaced by paparazzi, headlines such as *'Kylie Jenner breaks the internet with makeup free quarantine photos'* (2020) and *'Kylie Jenner makeup: the lockdown has revealed the real her'* appeared plentiful (Prance, 2020). With article follow up statements such as 'all that glitters, is not gold' and advice ordering girls not to step outside their house empowered by Jenner, it is no wonder women succumb to societal pressures.

As established in chapter one, images communicate messages that are translated into behavioural cues. Williamson (1978) argues that advertising companies provide a structure in which 'they are selling us ourselves'. Women view what is portrayed in the media and strive to aim for identical results by investing in the products models are bombarding them with. Bakhtin calls this method of manipulation an 'ideological performance' (McCormack, 2021). In semiotics, Barthes proposed the term 'myth' for images which adhere to a universal message, and subsequently their connotations appear denotive (Laughey, 2007). The depiction of recent Western beauty can be categorised as a myth as it encourages youthful, smooth, thin bodies, implying if one has or gains these qualities, they too will be considered beautiful.

Roberta Breitmore was a victim of the narrow-minded media as the popular models of the late twentieth century comprised of pencil-thin Twiggy, teen-model Brooke Shields (who released a celebrity-doll) and Kate Moss who pioneered the style 'heroin chic' - solidifying her stance on the dangerously low-weight trend by professing 'nothing tastes as good as skinny feels' (Costello, 2009). These models were all discovered when children or young teens. With many models fronting magazines with their prepubescent bodies, Roberta, aged thirty-one at the time of her psychiatric evaluation, could not compete with images of such youth.

In 2012, a UK inquiry revealed that 75% of respondents specified that celebrity culture, media and advertising were the prime social influences on their perception of body image, and subsequently, nearly ten million women feel significantly unhappy because of their appearance (All Party Parliamentary, 2012). Fransella and Crisp (1974) identified that women who were of a normal weight for their BMI, but still expressed dissatisfaction with their current weight compared to their ideal weight, revealed a discrepancy between their view of themselves versus their ideal self, which could lead to them being diagnosed as neurotic.

> A culture fixated on female thinness is not an obsession about female beauty, but an obsession about female obedience. Dieting is the most potent political sedative in women's history; a quietly mad population is a tractable one' (Wolf, 1991, p.187).

One-in-eight adults living in the UK have experienced suicidal thoughts due to body image anxieties (Mental Health Foundation, 2019). Roberta wished for, but couldn't achieve an optimum weight and so she became miserable. Breitmore contemplated suicide on the Golden Gate Bridge as a surveillance photo documents. Seligman (1975, p.184) writes 'the cause of depression is the belief that action is futile'.

Alarmingly, the purpose of the Beauty Myth is that it simply cannot be achieved, because there is always a new level of unhappiness for women to face, and it simply exists as a gendered power structure.

Dana Leslie

Chapter 3

Cash, Commodity and Commercialisation:

The unreasonable importance of self-maintenance for women in contemporary society and the art world today

Historically, public images of nude women could only be found in museums as they were presented as high-art. Art historian, Catherine McCormack, tells the often-unknown history of female nude painting The *Rokeby Venus* (1647-1651) in her 2021 book *Women in the Picture: Women, Art and the Power of Looking*. The painting was lacerated by suffragette Mary Richardson after entering the National Gallery with a concealed knife in 1914. Richardson was arrested and branded a monster for ruining the beautiful artwork. McCormack highlights that Richardson's destructive actions were not ill-conceived, but rather a demonstration that an object portraying a naked woman was revered, and of greater-value than the real women who were still thought of as second-class citizens, as they were still not allowed to vote (McCormack, 2021).

In 1989 the anonymous, feminist art collective *Guerilla Girls,* released an edition of posters titled *Do Women Have to Be Naked to get into the Met Museum?* and it has been recreated twice since. Each poster features a naked woman facing away from the viewer, exposing their backside, whilst wearing a gorilla mask and is accompanied by that year's Met Museum statistics. In 1989 the percentage of nude artwork portraying women in the Met was 85%, by 2005 this was 83% and 76% in 2012. However, the percentage of modern art created by women on display in the museum was less than 5% in 1989, 3% in 2005 and 4% in 2012. This reinforces John Berger's (1972, p.43) claim that 'men act and women appear' and women, being aware of this universal truth, watch themselves being looked at by men; turning themselves into an object.

The performance artist Marina Abramović acknowledges this unfair parallel for female artists in her 24-minute piece *Art Must Be Beautiful, Artist Must Be Beautiful* (1975). Abramović,, naked, viciously brushes her hair inflicting pain on herself, whilst repeating the words in the performance's title as though a mantra. Abramović is suffering for her art, mirroring life, and curator Jovana Stokić states she is commenting on 'the commodification of art and artist by critiquing conventions of and demands for female beauty in art and contemporary culture' (Biesenbach, 2010, p.25). Abramović has scarcely commented on the performance but has noted '[Art] beautiful or not beautiful is not important, it has to be true' (Kim, 2010).

John Berger posed the question 'what is a love of art?' and translated it to mean a 'desire to possess' stating 'if you buy a painting, you buy also the look of the thing it represents' (Berger, 1972, p.84). Buying a painting of the female nude grants the buyer power to look at her body whenever he pleases. After the development of the camera, mass-production of images became possible and the female nude was no longer confined to paintings. The pornography industry boomed and men's magazines, such as *Playboy*, cemented their place in culture, starting a new age of hyper-sexualised imagery in the mainstream media.

Berger (1972, p.125) believed 'publicity is the process of manufacturing glamour'. The Oxford English Dictionary (2022) defines glamour as 'beauty or charm that is sexually attractive'. Images are a form of promotion; they establish personal worth through being seen and consumed.

Paris Hilton changed the definition of a celebrity from being in the public eye due to talent, to simply just being in the public eye. Drew Pinsky observes 'she's most famous for being famous' (Pinsky, 2009, p.1). Hilton would alert paparazzi of her whereabouts, guaranteeing that photos of her would appear in the press ('Trainwreck', 2020). However, issues of *Nuts Magazine* featuring unknown glamour-models sold better than ones with unattainable celebrities on the front cover (Walter, 2009). Reality TV, such as *Big Brother*, gave ordinary women access to constant publicity. When commenting on why so many *Big Brother* excontestants turn to glamour-modelling, creative director Phil Edgar-Jones stated:

> The oddest people end up in newspapers in their bikinis...if it is a choice between that, and the glamour of that, and the financial rewards of that, and working in Superdrug for the rest of your life, well, kind of, why not? (Walter, 2009, p.31).

If beauty equals publicity and publicity equals money, a woman's body is proven to be an investment as though it is a 'currency system like the gold standard' as declared in *The Beauty Myth* (Wolf, 1991, p.7). In 2014, *The Sun* ran a Fantasy Football competition. The prize was not a standard product or cash reward but a woman. The winner would receive a date with one of the Page 3 glamour models of their choosing, objectifying women in order to 'possess' them as though a commodity. However, it is not just the media that capitalises on sexualising women's bodies. In 2015 an advertisement campaign for Cardiff buses flaunted topless women holding signs stating 'ride me all day for £3' (Cresci,

2015). The women in these advertisements do not need to compete against men for jobs in this field, men are their consumers. If a bus company can exploit the female body to gain exposure and increase sales, every industry can.

The ideal woman is silent, complaisant and beautiful. Women are reduced to images and images diminish the successful careers and accomplishments of women everywhere. Naomi Wolf writes 'every woman knows that, regardless of all her other achievements, she is a failure if she is not beautiful' (Wolf, 1991, p.23). A contemporary example of this is the societal reaction to singer-songwriter Adele's recent weight loss. Adele's numerous accolades distinguish her as one of the most successful musicians in history, despite this, the media's focus remains around the singer's weight, forcing her to clarify 'I don't make music for eyes, I make music for ears' (Touré, 2011). When news broke in 2020 that Adele had lost over a hundred pounds, the response quickly glorified such a feat, praising her 'glow up' - with some news outlets even branding it a 'revenge body' – despite Adele stating the weight loss was a result of her anxiety and she was 'addicted to working out' (Hattersley, 2021). The message this gives her 48.2 million Instagram followers is that her fifteen Grammy awards are not her greatest accomplishment, nor what makes her a successful artist, but rather her ability to shed the weight that was keeping her outside of celebrity culture.

Similarly, it was confirmed that Renée Zellweger was pulled off the cover of *Vogue* in the early 2000s due to gaining weight for her role in *Bridget Jones's Diary* - a career move that won her an Oscar (Betts, 2002). *Vogue's* priority was not to showcase talent as talent does not sell; images of women conforming to the beauty myth do. Wolf develops this theory further:

> Whenever we dismiss or do not hear a woman on television or in print because our attention has been drawn to her size or makeup or clothing or hairstyle, the beauty myth is working with optimum efficiency (Wolf, 1991, p.274).

Susan Boyle was almost laughed out of her *Britain's Got Talent* audition in 2009 after declaring she was aged 47 and wanted to be like Elaine Paige. The judges and audience blatantly dismissed Boyle, assuming that based on her appearance she would not be a talented singer. On hearing Boyle's extraordinary voice, host Ant McPartlin remarks on this bias 'you didn't expect that did you?' (Britain's Got Talent, 2019, 1:40).

Winner of *The Masked Singer* and ex-Girls Aloud band member, Nicola Roberts, has addressed this saddening truth for famous women, admitting she felt 'liberated' when singing behind the mask as it enabled her to do what she loves, without having to worry about hair, makeup, and lighting (Glynn, 2020). However, it's not just superstars that are held to high standards of self-presentation, because any woman who finds herself in the limelight is targeted with belittling comments in order to undermine their power. The Daily Mail headline *Never Mind Brexit, Who Won Leg-sit!* compares Nicola Sturgeon and Theresa May's choice to wear skirts to work as 'unsheathing' their 'finest weapons'

(Vine, 2017). And Marcia Clark, lead prosecutor in the O.J. Simpson murder case, found herself in the centre of a media circus, with the defence actively diminishing her creditability. She was ridiculed due to her appearance - Clark had a low-maintenance perm as she had young children at home - and was subjected to a segment called *Marcia Clark: Bitch or Babe?* on The Beat Radio Show (Darden, 1996). Clark's outdated topless photos on a nude beach were sold and published during the trial, ruining her reputation and leading newspapers to call her an unfit mother. As Clark was a practical, career-driven mother, she was not seen as desirable and therefore men did not want to own her nude photos. Female power and success are not the result of women cultivating their minds but rather investing hours into their outward appearances: neither talent nor intellect is championed in a sexist society.

From 1984-1989 The Turner Prize was awarded to white, middle-aged men; the oldest, Malcolm Morley and Howard Hodgkin, were fifty-three and the youngest was Tony Cragg at age thirty-nine. In 1990 there was no prize due to a lack of sponsorship (Lubbock, 2007). The following year, the Tate announced the Turner Prize would have an upper age limit of fifty. Dr Helen Gorrill links youth, celebrity culture and mainstream media to artists in the 1990s, when Tate's decision was made. In *Women Can't Paint* (2020) Gorrill quotes art historian Julian Stalabrass:

> An emphasis on the image of youth, the prevalence of work that reproduces well on magazine pages, and the rise of the celebrity artist; work that cosies up to commodity culture and the fashion industry, and serves as accessible honey pots to sponsors (Foster, 2008 as cited in Gorrill, 2020, p.137).

The decision to implement an upper age limit was to appeal to younger audiences in order to attract sponsors. Subsequently, five out of the nine winners in the 90s were known as part of *Young British Artists,* all of whom were in their early thirties. In 1999 one nominee garnered a lot of attention for the award but did not win. Gorrill (2020, p.137) states 'Tracey Emin is a YBA who slid easily into the role of young artist-as-celebrity, surrounded by an enticing aura of youth, sexuality and glamour'. Emin was branded the artworlds 'bad-girl' by media condemning her artistic and behavioural antics (Longrigg, 1997).

In 1998 Emin, known for her autobiographical artworks, created the piece *My Bed*, exhibiting her own bed in which she had suffered a four-day breakdown. The items she had interacted with during this state left a messy self-portrait in her wake. Alongside the unmade bed and its dirty sheets were menstrual blood-stained underwear, used tissues and condoms, packets of contraceptive pills, empty vodka bottles, cigarette butts, slippers, lube and a pregnancy test; left as though the remnants of a performance. *My Bed* was controversial, although many had celebrated Marcel Duchamp's revolutionary Readymades (Chalupecký and Wilson, 1985), art critics reacted unfavourably to Emin's piece. David Lee writes in his review 'she can't paint, she can't draw and she can't sculpt...*My Bed* is stillborn artistically' (Barnett, 2000). Duchamp is innovative and radical; Emin is talentless and unsuccessful.

Donnell (1999, p.124) states 'the explosion of criticism surrounding autobiography, and particularly women's autobiography…has demonstrated that as a genre autobiography can be likened to a restless and unmade bed'.

In 2007, *Nuts Magazine* ran a 'Babes on the Bed' competition, looking for the next undiscovered glamour model to push magazine sales. The advert informs glamour model Lucy Pinder will present, exclaiming she 'loves her bed' as it's the 'best place to have sex'. The text is accompanied by a photo of Pinder wearing only a thong and a thin, clean, white bed sheet barely covering her nipples. Her body is tanned, slender, hairless and smooth and her hair drapes perfectly. She is wearing large hoop earrings and a full face of make-up to emanate the myth that all women look like this when lying in bed – an image a far cry from reality.

Emin could be no further from *Nuts* desired 'Babes on the Bed' fad. The unspoken social decorum for a female's private life had been shattered. Emin was not sexualising her body for men to imagine and idolise being with, but exposing the realistic, messy aftermath of having intimate relationships. The decaying mess the artist had encompassed herself with demystified her as an object and unveiled her declining mental state. Neither of these elements are seen as glamourous and, as *My Bed* was an extension of Emin herself, the value of her art was attached to her image, which consequently was not seen as high-value as other artists.

Duchamp's assisted Readymade *Belle Haleine, Eau de Voilette* (1921) - a perfume bottle featuring an image of the artist's female persona - sold for €8.9 million (Christie's, 2009). Emin's *My Bed* which uncovered her guise as a woman celebrity, sold for less than a third of Duchamp's (Grimbergen, 2014).

Emin - like Ukeles and Hershman Leeson - combined her life and art, exposing truths which surround female identity – and, of course, the value attached to a woman's image.

Dana Leslie

Conclusion

Throughout recent historical feminist art practice, female artists have reflected the inequality they faced in the artworld and society, shifting their practice in relation to contemporary forms of oppression.

During the second wave of feminism women were delegated all housework chores, allowing men the privilege to work and earn their own money without having to maintain the household. Women were without freedom and time and so could not pursue their own endeavours outside of the home. Advertisements fuelled the outdated belief systems helping create and maintain the myth of women as housewife, man as breadwinner – the effects of which are still being felt decades later. Artists such as Ukeles critique the disparity between both man and woman, and artist and woman artist, through using their art as a medium to allow for discussion and change.

After feminists gained access to the workforce, beauty work superseded housework, and self-maintenance became the new injustice placed upon women. Women are taught young that if they adhere to gender-norm expectations they will receive praise, to the extent that females deforming themselves through unhealthy dieting, harsh exercise regimes, cosmetic surgery and superficial, expensive beauty treatments have become the norm. Women are familiar that those who do not comply with such expectations will not be granted success, however there is no equivalent with males as they are largely, and arguably the ones who hold the power to censor and publish images of men. The media reinforces beauty myths through their choice of models and ads. Women are forced to survey themselves constantly and because the unrealistic standards can never be met, half the population becomes miserable, or at least pre-occupied. Lynn Hershman Leeson's fabricated persona showcases this sad reality for many women in Western society, confirming Beauvoir's argument that a woman is created and not a natural entity.

Women who conform to the beauty myth, are looked at. Through maintaining their appearance, women can become possessable objects or sellable commodities for other companies. Sexual imagery sells and even the most unlikely establishments can succumb to using such methods to secure sponsorship and profits. Women, including female artists, are viewed intertwined with their appearance; the value of their work and body correlates. The *YBAs* helped garner attention and secure money for large art institutions, however did not necessarily benefit with equal compensation. Tracey Emin's autobiographical artworks are often discredited by critics who have consumed her image in the press. Women who portray themselves sexually and inviting are glorified as they upkeep male expectations, career women who ignore these wants of their consumers will not be as successful, as men are not benefitting from their work.

The disadvantages women faced from the 1960s onwards are still relevant today. Without the work of the female artists and authors discussed, women would not be able to critique their institutions and cultures.

Feminist art, therefore, creates discussion and subverts expectations, exploring - and subsequently widening - the category of gender roles for the better.

References

All Party Parliamentary Group (2012). 'Reflections on Body Image'. *All Party Parliamentary Group and YMCA Central.* Available at: http://ymca-central-assets.s3-eu-west-1.amazonaws.com/s3fs-public/APPG-Reflections-on-body-image.pdf (Accessed 22 December 2021).

AOL/Today (2014). 'Ideal to Real Body Image Survey'. *AOL.com and Today.com.* Available at: https://www.aol.com/article/2014/02/24/loveyourselfie/20836450/?guccounter=1&guce_referrer=aHR0cHM6Ly93d3cuZ29vZ2xlLmNvbS8&guce_referrer_sig=AQAAAM7YfQIwps-NQec3_5jG3m19lLM1TEu7g3L0AuJ8UnaH63CjBjvx-CnahkqjQPMGTtUNwwQJ2YrlxowpWgK5ztb3QX7089orLl7g8nUNMx3PYpi8rcFs8rti1nztMFBa0CZg-u5MdNwTKIfDVgCkBKCvgJpkcfGOk7BH6TgBRYu4 (Accessed 22 December 2021).

Archard et al. (2017). 'Cosmetic Procedures: Ethical Issues', *Nuffield Council on Bioethics.* London. Available at: https://www.nuffieldbioethics.org/assets/pdfs/Cosmetic-procedures-full-report.pdf (Accessed 27 December 2021).

Barnett, A. (2000). 'Tracey made the bed. Now Saatchi can lie in it', *The Guardian,* 16 July. Available at: https://www.theguardian.com/uk/2000/jul/16/antony barnett.theobserver (Accessed 4 January 2022).

Bates, L. (2018). *Misogynation: The True Scale of Sexism.* London: Simon & Schuster.

Beauvoir, S. (2011). *The Second Sex.* Translated from French by C. Borde and S. Malovany-Chevallier. New York: Alfred A. Knopf.

Berger, J. (1972). *Ways of seeing.* New York, NY: Viking.

Betts, K. (2002). 'The Tyranny of Skinny, Fashion's Insider Secret', *The New York Times*, 31 March. Available at: https://www.nytimes.com/2002/03/31/style/the-tyranny-of-skinny-fashion-s-insider-secret.html (Accessed 2 January 2022).

Biesenbach, K. (2010). *Marina Abramovic: The Artist Is Present.* 1st ed. New York: Museum of Modern Art.

Bott, E. (1957). *Family and Social Network.* London: Tavistock Publications.

Britain's Got Talent (2019). *Susan Boyle's First Audition 'I Dreamed a Dream' Britain's Got Talent,* 7 March. Available at: https://www.youtube.com/watch?v=yE1Lxw5ZyXk&ab_channel=Britain%27sGotTalent (Accessed 2 January 2022).

Butler, J. (1988). 'Performative Acts and Gender Constitution: An Essay in Phenomenology and Feminist Theory', *Theatre Journal*, 40(4), pp.519–531, doi:10.2307/3207893.

Carlson, R. (1970). 'On the Structure of Self-Esteem: Comments on Ziller's Formulation'. *Journal of Consulting and Clinical Psychology,* 34, pp.264-268.

Chalupecký, J. and Wilson, P. (1985). 'Marcel Duchamp: A Re-Evaluation', *Artibus et Historiae*, 6(11), pp. 125–36, doi:10.2307/1483262.

Chicago, J. (1982). *Through the Flower: My Struggle as a Woman Artist* London: The Women's Press.

Christie's (2006). 'Christie's pays tribute to a 20th century style icon in September', *Christies.com*, 10 August. Available at: https://www.christies.com/presscenter/pdf/08212006/123312.pdf (Accessed 24 December 2021).

Christie's (2009). '2009 Live Auction 1209 Collection Yves Saint Laurent et Pierre Bergé: Lot 37; Marcel Duchamp (1887-1968) Belle Haleine - Eau De Voilette', *Christies.com*, 25 February. Available at: https://www.christies.com/lot/lot-5157362?ldp_breadcrumb=back&intObjectID=5157362&from=salessummary&lid=1 (Accessed 4 January 2022).

Correa, D. (2009). 'The Construction of Gender Identity: A Semiotic Analysis', *Race, Ethnicity and Gender in Education*. Springer Netherlands, pp. 183-194, doi: 10.1007/978-1-4020-9739-3_10.

Costello, B. (2009). 'Kate Moss: The Waif That Roared'. *WWD Fashion*, 13 November. Available at: http://www.wwd.com/beauty-industry-news/kate-moss-the-waif-that-roared-2367932//?full=true (Accessed 17 December 2021).

Cresci, E. (2015). 'Bus company pulls topless 'ride me' adverts after outcry', *The Guardian*, 11 May. Available at: https://www.theguardian.com/media/2015/may/11/bus-company-pulls-topless-ride-me-adverts-after-outcry (Accessed 30 December 2021

Darden, C. (1996). *In Contempt*. New York: HarperCollins.

Davies, F. (1933). 'Wife of the Master Mural Painter Gleefully Dabbles in Works of Art', *The Detroit News*. Available at: https://www.openculture.com/2015/03/1933-article-on-frida-kahlo-wife-of-the-master-mural-painter-gleefully-dabbles-in-works-of-art.html (Accessed 17 December 2021).

Dominick, J. and Rauch, G. (1972). The Image of Women in Network TV Commercials'. *Journal of Broadcasting*, 16(3), pp.259-266.

Donnell, A. (1999). 'When Writing the Other Is Being True to the Self: Jamaica Kincaid's "The Autobiography of My Mother"' in Polkey, P. (ed.) *Women's Lives into Print: The Theory, Practice and Writing of Feminist Auto/Biography*. London: MacMillan; New York: St. Martin's.

Eriksson, U. (2010). Extract of *Mary Kelly Four Works in Dialogue 1973-2010*, *The British Library*. Available at: http://www.bl.uk/learning/histcitizen/sisterhood/clips/culture-and-the-arts/visual-arts/143927.html (Accessed 3 January 2022).

Fawcett Society. (2020). *Equal Pay Day: UK At a "Coronavirus Crossroads" On Gender Equality*. London: Fawcett Society. Available at: https://www.fawcettsociety.org.uk/news/equal-pay-day-uk-at-a-coronavirus-crossroads-on-gender-equality (Accessed 18 December 2021).

Fawcett Society. (2021). *The Impact of the Coronavirus Pandemic on Disabled Parents* London: Fawcett Society. Available at: https://www.fawcettsociety.org.uk/Handlers/Download.ashx?IDMF=75fecbfb-858f-42da-b887-1966f384db02 (Accessed 18 December 2021).

Finkelpearl, T. (2001). *Dialogues in Public Art*. Cambridge: MIT Press.

Firestone, S. (1979). *The Dialectic of Sex: The Case for Feminist Revolution*. London: Women's Press.

Fiske, J. (1990). 'Ideology and Meanings'. In *Introduction to Communication Studies*. London: Routledge.

Fransella, F. and Frost, K. (1977). *On Being a Woman: Review of Research on How Women See Themselves*. London: Tavistock.

Friedan, B. (1963). *The Feminine Mystique*. New York: W. W. Norton & Company.

Gauntlett, D. (2002). *Media, Gender and Identity*. London: Routledge.

Gimenez, M. (2005). 'Capitalism and the Oppression of Women: Marx Revisited'. *Science & Society*, *69*(1), 11–32. Available at: http://www.jstor.org/stable/40404227 (Accessed: 27 December 2021).

Glynn, P. (2020). 'Nicola Roberts: "I was nervous to take the mask off"', *BBC News*, 17 February. Available at: https://www.bbc.co.uk/news/entertainment-arts-51532071 (Accessed 2 January 2022).

Gorrill, H. (2020). *Women Can't Paint: Gender, the Glass Ceiling and Values in Contemporary Art.* London: Bloomsbury.

Greer, G. (1986). *The Female Eunuch.* London: Grafton Books.

Greer, G. (2007). *The Whole Woman.* London: Black Swan.

Gregory, J. (1808). *A Father's Legacy to His Daughters.* London: T. Cadell and W. Davies.

Gregos, K. (2011). 'The Importance of Being Roberta'. Available at: https://www.shanghartgallery.com/galleryarchive/texts/id/8827 (Accessed 22 December 2021).

Grimbergen, D. van (2014) '2014 Live Auction 1535 Post-War & Contemporary Art Evening Auction: Lot 19; Tracey Emin (B. 1963) My Bed', *Christies.com*, 1 July 2014. Available at: https://www.christies.com/lot/lot-tracey-emin-my-bed-5813479/?from=salesummary&intObjectID=5813479&sid=33189f7a-11cf-4cb7-a06d-f5296c14c390 (Accessed 4 January 2022)

Groskop, V. (2015). '*Tracey Emin:* "I'm not flaky and I don't compromise"', *Red Online,* 14 October. Available at: https://www.redonline.co.uk/red-women/interviews/a506662/tracey-emin-interview/ (Accessed 27 December 2021).

Hari, J. (2012). 'It costs me a lot of money to look this cheap', Evening Standard. 5 April. Available at: https://www.standard.co.uk/showbiz/it-costs-me-a-lot-of-money-to-look-this-cheap-6696737.html (Accessed: 24 December 2021).

Harrison, C. and Wood, P. (2003). *Art in Theory, 1900 - 2000: An Anthology of Changing Ideas.* 2nd ed. Malden: Blackwell Publishing.

Hattersley, G. (2021). 'Adele, Reborn: The British Icon Gets Candid About Divorce, Body Image, Romance & Her "Self-Redemption" Record', *British Vogue (November).* Available at: https://www.vogue.co.uk/arts-and-lifestyle/article/adele-british-vogue-interview (Accessed 1 January 2022).

Hernadon, P. (1991). *Family Life Among the Ashanti of West Africa.* Available at: https://teachersinstitute.yale.edu/curriculum/units/1991/2/91.02.04.x.html (Accessed: 20 December 2021).

Hershman Leeson, L. (1996). 'Romancing the Anti-body: Lust and Longing in (Cyber)space'. In *Clicking In: Hot Links to a Digital Culture.* Seattle: Bay Press, pp.329-345.

Hershman Leeson, L. and Weibel, P. (2016). *Lynn Hershman Leeson: Civic Radar.* Ostfildern: Hatje Cantz.

Jacob, M and Roth, M. (1983). *The Amazing Decade: Women and performance art in America, 1970-1980.* Los Angeles: Astro Artz.

Joseph, C. (2021). 'William Dorsey Swann'. *Oxford African American Studies Centre: African American National Biography*. Available at: https://www.academia.edu/49043126/William_Dorsey_Swann_Oxford_African_American_Studies_Center (Accessed 29 December 2021).

Keeps, D. (1993). 'Pop View; How RuPaul Ups the Ante for Drag', *The New York Times,* 11 July. Available at: https://www.nytimes.com/1993/07/11/archives/pop-view-how-rupaul-ups-the-ante-for-drag.html (Accessed 29 December 2021).

Kim, H. (2010). 'Listening to Marina Abramović: *Art Must Be Beautiful, Artist Must Be Beautiful*', *Moma.org,* 6 April. Available at: https://www.moma.org/explore/inside_out/2010/04/06/listening-to-marina-abramovic-art-must-be-beautiful-artist-must-be-beautiful/ (Accessed 30 December 2021).

'Kylie Jenner breaks the internet with makeup free quarantine photos' (2020), *Whattolaugh.com*, Available at: https://www.whattolaugh.com/kylie-jenner-without-makeup-2020/ (Accessed 29 December 2021).

Lacey, M. (2012). '"Don't eat!": Controversial 1965 Slumber Party Barbie came with scales permanently set to just 110lbs and a diet book telling her not to eat', *Mail Online*, 29 November. Available at: https://www.dailymail.co.uk/femail/article-2239931/1965-Slumber-Party-Barbie-came-scales-set-110lbs-diet-book-telling-eat.html (Accessed: 24 December 2021).

Laughey, D. (2007). *Key Themes in Media Theory*. Maidenhead: Open University Press.

Liss, A. (2009). *Feminist Art and the Maternal*. Minneapolis: University of Minnesota Press.

Longrigg, C. (1997). 'Sixty Minutes, Noise: by art's bad girl', *The Guardian*, 4 December, Available at: https://www.theguardian.com/artanddesign/1997/dec/04/20yearsoftheturnerprize.turnerprize1 (Accessed 3 January 2022).

Lopata, H. (1971). *Occupation: Housewife*. New York: Oxford University Press.

Lubbock, T. (2007). 'What's the point of the Turner Prize?', *The Independent*, 2 October. Available at: https://www.independent.co.uk/news/uk/this-britain/what-s-the-point-of-the-turner-prize-395747.html (Accessed 3 January 2022).

McCormack, C. (2021). *Women in the Picture: Women, Art and the Power of Looking*. London: Icon Books Ltd.

Mee, D and Wong, B (2012). 'Facial Plastic Surgery', *Medical Makeup for Concealing Facial Scars*, 28(5), pp.536-540, doi:10.1055/s-0032-1325647.

Mental Health Foundation (2019). 'Body Image: How we think and feel about our bodies'. London: Mental Health Foundation. Available at: https://www.mentalhealth.org.uk/sites/default/files/DqVNbWRVvpAPQzw.pdf (Accessed 24 December 2021).

Mumsnet. HQ. (2019). '96% of mothers agree having children affects women's careers for the worse', *Mumsnet,* 1 June. Available at: https://www.mumsnet.com/articles/career-break-returners/ (accessed 18 December 2021).

Nochlin, L. (2021). *Why Have There Been No Great Women Artists? 50th Anniversary Edition.* London: Thames & Hudson.

Oakley, A. (1974). *The Sociology of Housework.* London: Martin Robertson.

Oxford Online Dictionary (2022). Definition of '*glamour'*. Available at: https://www.lexico.com/definition/glamour (Accessed 2 January 2022).

Parker, R. and Pollock, G. (1987) *Framing Feminism: Art and the Women's Movement 1970-85.* London: Pandora.

Perraudin, F. (2015). 'Cameron hits back at Tory MP's "outrageous" maternity leave comments', *The Guardian,* 23 February. Available at: https://www.theguardian.com/money/2015/feb/23/cameron-hits-back-tory-mps-out-maternity-leave-comments-rachel-reeves-andrew-rosindell (Accessed 18 December 2021).

Pinsky, Drew. (2009). *The Mirror Effect: How Celebrity Narcissism Is Seducing America.* 1st ed. New York: Harper.

Prance, S. (2020). 'Kylie Jenner breaks the internet with makeup free quarantine photos', *Popbuzz,* 22 April, Available at: https://www.popbuzz.com/celeb/kylie-jenner-makeup-free-quarantine-look/ (Accessed 29 December 2021).

Ramli, N. (2015). 'Immigrant Entrepreneurs on the World's Successful Global Brands in the Cosmetic Industry', *Procedia, Social and Behavioral Sciences*, 195, pp. 113–122. doi:10.1016/j.sbspro.2015.06.417.

Rebel Women: The Great Art Fight Back (2018). Directed by Clare Tavernor. 18 June, BBC Four. Available at: Box of Broadcasts (Accessed 28 December 2021).

Roberts, Y. (1989). 'Standing Up to Be Counted', *The Guardian*. London.

Rousseau, J. (1762). *Emile, or On Education*. Translated from French by B. Foxley, 1921. London & Toronto: J.M. Dent and Sons; New York: E.P. Dutton.

Roy, A. (1998). 'Images of domesticity and motherhood in Indian television commercials: A critical study'. *Journal of Popular Culture*, 32(3), pp. 117-134. doi:10.1111/j.0022-3840.1998.3203_117.x.

Seligman, M. (1975). *Helplessness: On Depression, Development and Death*. New York: W. H. Freeman & Co.

Siegler, M. (2017). 'T. J. Miller's wife making a name for herself in New York', *Page Six,* 24 June. Available at: https://pagesix.com/2017/06/24/tj-millers-wife-making-a-name-for-herself-in-new-york/ (Accessed 17 December 2021).

Sladen, M. (1995). 'Allen Jones', *Frieze*, 23 (June/August). Available at: https://www.frieze.com/article/allen-jones (Accessed 28 December 2021).

Tavris, C. (1973). 'Who Likes Women's Liberation - and Why?: The Case of the Unliberated Liberals'. *Journal of Social Issues*. 29, pp.175-198. doi: 10.1111/j.1540-4560.1973.tb00110.x.

Touré (2011). 'Adele Opens Up About Her Inspirations, Looks and Stage Fright', *Rolling Stone*, 1129, 28 April. Available at: https://www.rollingstone.com/music/music-news/adele-opens-up-about-her-inspirations-looks-and-stage-fright-79626/ (Accessed 1 January 2022).

'Trainwreck' (2020). *Celebrity: A 21st-Century Story*, episode 2, 30 December. BBC Two. Available at: Box of Broadcasts (Accessed 30 November 2021).

Vine, S. (2017). 'One was relaxed, every inch a stateswoman while her opposite number was tense and uncomfortable: Sarah Vine says May v Sturgeon was a knockout victory for the PM', *Daily Mail*, 28 March. Available at: https://www.dailymail.co.uk/debate/article-4354996/SARAH-VINE-says-v-Sturgeon-victory-PM.html (Accessed 2 January 2022).

Walker Art Centre (1977). *Untitled from Roberta's Internal Transformations: Language from Roberta [open page from diary] by Lynn Hershman Leeson*. Available at: http://walkerart.org/collections/artworks/untitled-from-robertas-internal-transformations-language-from-roberta-open-page-from-diary (Accessed 20 December 2021).

Walker Art Centre (1978). *Untitled from Roberta's Internal Transformations: Language from Roberta [excerpt from Roberta's psychiatric evaluation] by Lynn Hershman Leeson.* Available at: https://walkerart.org/collections/artworks/untitled-from-robertas-internal-transformations-language-from-roberta-excerpt-from-robertas-psychiatric-evaluation (Accessed 20 December 2021).

Walter, N. (2011). *Living Dolls: The Return of Sexism.* 2nd ed. London: Virago Press.

Williamson, J, (1978). *Decoding Advertisements: Ideology and Meaning in Advertising.* London: Marion Boyars.

Wolf, N. (1991). *The Beauty Myth: How Images of Beauty Are Used Against Women.* London, Vintage.

Zapata, M. (2016). 'The Horrifying Legacy of the Victorian Tapeworm Diet', *Atlas Obscura.* 26 October. Available at: https://www.atlasobscura.com/articles/the-horrifying-legacy-of-the-victorian-tapeworm-diet (Accessed 22 December 2021).

Dana Leslie

Glossary

Assisted Readymade 'refers to works of this type [see Readymade definition] whose components have been combined or modified by the artist' (MoMA, 2022).

Beauty Myth 'an obsession with physical perfection that traps the modern woman in an endless spiral of hope, self-consciousness, and self-hatred as she tries to fulfil society's impossible definition of "the flawless beauty."' (Wolf, 1991, blurb). Coined by writer Naomi Wolf she states it is the 'last, best belief system that keeps male dominance intact' (Wolf, 1991, pp.12).

Commodification 'the action of process of treating a person or thing a property which can be traded or whose value is purely monetary' (Oxford English Dictionary as cited in Hermann, 2021) 'anything intended for exchange' (Ertman and Williams, 2005, p35).

Cultural Determinism 'is defined as a reaction against the biological determinism' (Dutton, 2018). Individual's behaviour and characteristics constructed through culture – 'socially shared and transmitted system of norms, values, and ideas of a social group, or, as some prefer, its "meaning systems."… The culture of a social group can be distinguished from the patterned social relations that characterise its various institutional domains-economic, political, familial, and so on. (Spiro, 2001).

Feminine 'having qualities or an appearance traditionally associated with women' (Oxford English Dictionary, 2022a).

Feminist Art 'art that reveals the nature of women's private experience, in order to influence cultural attitudes and transform stereotypes…change [is the] goal' (Lacy, 1991).

Gender 'is a social concept referring to psychologically, sociologically, or culturally rooted traits, attitudes, beliefs, and behavioural tendencies…[Gender] is not fully determined by sex' (Bristor and Fischer, 1993, p.519).

Gender Identity 'one's innermost concept of self as male, female, a blend of both or neither – how individuals perceive themselves and what they call themselves. One's gender identity can be the same or different from their sex assigned at birth' (Human Rights Campaign, 2022).

'Glow up' variation of '"glo up", which was coined in August 2013 by rapper Chief Keef in the song Gotta Glo Up One Day and later gained traction as an expression to describe an impressive personal transformation' (Shoemark, 2020).

Gynaeceum 'the inner section of a house, used as women's quarters' (Collins Online Dictionary, 2022).

'Heroin Chic' 'an extremely thin physique paired with pale skin, dark undereye circles, and often dishevelled hair and clothing' (Nolen, 2010). 'Emerged in the 1990s as a high-class fashion trend which appropriated visual imagery of heroin junkies and their environment into fashion photography' (Rosser, 2010).

Heteronormative 'the assumption that heterosexuality is the default, preferred, 'normal' state for human beings because of the belief that people fall into one or other category of a strict gender binary. Thus, it involves the further assumption that someone's biological sex, sexuality, gender identity, and gender roles are aligned' (Harris and White, 2018, p.335).

Hyper-sexualised 'the proliferation of suggestively or explicitly pornographic images in mainstream society…overt or explicit sexuality/sexualization…in tandem with cultures shifting views and visual acceptance of pornography in post-modern society. It is the degree to which sexuality is being utilised in contemporary advertising that it is no longer used to entice or provoke viewers. Instead, imagery is generated to not only command, but to also stimulate and titillate a gaze that has been brought forth by the proliferation and mainstreaming of soft- core pornography' (Mace, 2012).

Ideological Performance 'the dramaturgical aspects…within social movements, both publicly and privately…woven into everyday lives which [influences] the formation and maintenance of collective identity at the level of interaction. Use various cultural elements, including humour, boundary objects, understandings of the audience, language, and style, both consciously and unconsciously, situating performers and audiences within meaning systems and formulating collective identities' (Fuist, 2014).

Ideology 'system of beliefs and values that emanate from and promulgate the worldview of the dominant group in a society' (Hirshman, 1993, p.573).

Institutionalised Sexism 'refers to gender discrimination reflected in the policies and practices of organizations such as governments, corporations (workplaces), public institutions (schools, health care), and financial institutions. These practices derive from systemic sexist beliefs that women are inferior to and therefore less capable than men' (Capodilupo, 2017).

Maintenance 'the work needed to keep something in good condition' and 'a situation in which something continues to exist or is not allowed to become less' (Cambridge Online Dictionary, 2022a).

Male Gaze 'is where women in the media are viewed from the eyes of a heterosexual man, and that these women are represented as passive objects of male desire. Audiences are forced to view women from the point of view of a heterosexual male, even if they are heterosexual women or homosexual men' (Sampson, 2015).

Masculine 'having qualities or appearance traditionally associated with men' (Oxford Online Dictionary, 2022b).

Matrilineal 'relating to, based on, or tracing descent through the maternal line' (Merriam-Webster Online Dictionary, 2022a).

Myth Roland Barthes proposed the term for 'a semiological system which has the pretension of transcending itself into a factual system' (Barthes, 2000 p.134) and connotations of signs come to appear denotative (Laughey, 2007).

Oppression 'a situation in which people are governed in an unfair and cruel way and prevented from having opportunities and freedom' (Cambridge Online Dictionary, 2022b)

Patriarchy 'literally means the rule of the father or the "patriarch", and originally it was used to describe a specific type of "male-dominated family"' (Sultana, 2012). More recently, considered a broader term for 'a system of social structures, and practices in which men dominate, oppress and exploit women' (Walby, 1989, p214).

Persona 'describes the wider practice of constructing and constituting forms of public identity' (Barbour et al, 2015). Describes the wider practice of constructing and constituting forms of public identity.

Radical Feminist someone who is part of the 'political movement to end male supremacy in all areas of social and economic life, and rejects the whole idea of opposing male and female natures and values as a sexist idea' (Willis, 1984).

Readymade 'a term coined by Marcel Duchamp in 1916 to describe prefabricated, often mass-produced objects isolated from their intended use and elevated to the status of art by the artist choosing and designating them as such' (MoMA, 2022).

'Revenge-body' '[used for] asserting revenge on "haters" who made [a] chubby person feel bad about him or herself through overt criticism or romantic rejection' (Einstein et al, 2018,). Popularised after the 2017 reality TV show *Revenge Body with Khloé Kardashian* in which she states in every episode's title sequence 'a great body is the best revenge' (Revenge Body with *Khloé Kardashian*, 2017).

Second-wave Feminism 'movement that took place in the 1960s and 1970s and focused on issues of equality and discrimination. Starting initially in the United States with American women, the feminist liberation movement soon spread to other Western countries… Unfolding in the context of the anti-war and civil rights movement, the catalyst for second wave feminism was Betty Friedan's 1963 book, *The Feminine Mystique*, which criticized the post-war belief that a woman's role was to marry and bear children' (Second Wave Feminism, 2022).

Self-maintenance maintenance of the self: 'the act or process of maintaining oneself or itself' (Merriam-Webster Online Dictionary, 2022b). See definition for 'maintenance'.

Sex 'is a biological concept that allows us to distinguish between males and females purely on the basis of physiological characteristics' (Bristor and Fischer, 1993 p.519).

Slommack 'an awkward, uncouth, or slovenly person: slob' (Merriam-Webster Online Dictionary, 2022c).

Slut 'a promiscuous person: someone who has many sexual partners —usually used of a woman' (Merriam-Webster Online Dictionary, 2022d)

The Masked Singer ITV television show based on South Korean show *King of Mask Singer* which features a panel of judges assessing the anonymous 'singing competition, which sees 12 celebrities don masks to pull off performances' (White, 2019).

Young British Artists (YBAs) 'the label applied to a loose group of British artists who began to exhibit together in 1988 and who became known for their openness to materials and processes, shock tactics and entrepreneurial attitude' (Tate, 2022).

Dana Leslie

Glossary reference list

Barbour, K. et al. (2015). 'Persona as method: exploring celebrity and the public self through persona studies'. *Celebrity Studies*, 6, pp. 1-18. doi:10.1080/19392397.2015.1062649.

Barthes, R. (2000). *Mythologies*. London: Vintage Books.

Bristor, J.M. and Fischer, E. (1993). 'Feminist Thought: Implications for marketing research', *Journal of Consumer Research*, 19, pp. 518-536. Available at: http://www.jstor.org/stable/2489438 (Accessed 12 January 2022).

Cambridge Online Dictionary (2022a). Definition of 'maintenance'. Available at: https://dictionary.cambridge.org/dictionary/english/maintenance (Accessed 17 January 2022).

Cambridge Online Dictionary (2022b). Definition of 'oppression'. Available at: https://dictionary.cambridge.org/dictionary/english/oppression(Accessed 17 January 2022).

Capodilupo, C. (2017). 'Institutional Sexism'. In: Kevin L. Nadal Editor, 2017. *The SAGE Encyclopedia of Psychology and Gender*, pp. 941-942. doi:10.4135/9781483384269.n317> (Accessed 19 Jan 2022).

Collins Online Dictionary (2022). Definition of 'gynaeceum'. Available at: https://www.collinsdictionary.com/dictionary/english/gynaeceum (Accessed: 15 January 2022).

Dutton, E.C. (2022). 'Determinism, Cultural'. *The International Encyclopedia of Anthropology*, H. Callan (Ed.). doi:10.1002/9781118924396.wbiea1293.

Einstein, M. et al. (2018). 'Making over body and soul'. *Religion and Reality TV: Faith in Late Capitalism*. London: Routledge pp.34.

Ertman, M. and Williams, J (2005). *Rethinking Commodification: Cases and Readings in Law and Culture*, New York: New York University Press.

Fuist, T. (2014). 'The Dramatization of Beliefs, Values, and Allegiances: Ideological Performances Among Social Movement Groups and Religious Organizations', *Social Movement Studies*, 13(4), pp. 427-442. doi: 10.1080/14742837.2013.832189

Harris, J. and White, V. (2018). *A Dictionary of Social Work and Social Care*. Oxford: Oxford University Press.

Hermann, C. (2021). *The Critique of Commodification: Contours of a Post-Capitalist Society*. Oxford: Oxford University Press.

Hirschman, E.C. (1993). 'Ideology in Consumer Research 1980 and 1990: A Marxist and Feminist Critique', *Journal of Consumer Research*, 19, pp. 537-555.

Human Rights Campaign (2022). 'Glossary of Terms'. Available at: https://www.hrc.org/resources/glossary-of-terms (Accessed 13 January 2022).

Lacy, S. (1991). 'The Name of the Game'. *Art Journal*, 50(2), pp. 64–68. https://doi.org/10.2307/777165.

Mace, C. (2012). Mace, C., 2012. *Fashion or Porn?: the Hyper-Sexualization of Western Culture and the Commodification of Sex*. Master's thesis. Parsons the New School for Design. Available at: https://www.academia.edu/download/34423669/THESIS.doc.pdf (Accessed 15 January 2022).

Merriam-Webster Online Dictionary (2022a). Definition of 'matrilineal'. Available at: https://www.merriam-webster.com/dictionary/matrilineal (Accessed 15 Jan. 2022).

Merriam-Webster Online Dictionary (2022b). Definition of 'self-maintenance'. Available at: https://www.merriam-webster.com/dictionary/self-maintenance (Accessed 15 Jan. 2022).

Merriam-Webster Online Dictionary (2022c). Definition of 'slommack'. Available at: https://www.merriam-webster.com/dictionary/slommack (Accessed 15 Jan. 2022).

Merriam-Webster Online Dictionary (2022d). Definition of 'slut'. Available at: https://www.merriam-webster.com/dictionary/slut (Accessed 15 Jan. 2022).

MoMA (2022). 'Readymade', *MoMA*, Available at: https://www.moma.org/collection/terms/readymade (Accessed 15 January 2022).

Nolen, J. (2010). 'Gisele Bündchen', *Britannica.com*. Available at: https://www.britannica.com/biography/Gisele-Bundchen (Accessed 14 January 2022).

Oxford Online Dictionary (2022a). Definition of 'feminine'. Available at: https://www.lexico.com/definition/feminine (Accessed 14 January 2022)

Oxford Online Dictionary (2022b). Definition of 'masculine'. Available at: https://www.lexico.com/definition/masculine (Accessed 14 January 2022)

Revenge Body with Khloé Kardashian (2017). E!. Available at: Amazon Prime Video (Accessed 17 January 2022).

Rosser, E. M. 2010. 'Heroin Chic: The Fashion Phenomenon Analysed Through the Writing of Christine Harold and Timothy Hickman'. *Inquiries Journal/Student Pulse*, 2(12). Available at: http://www.inquiriesjournal.com/a?id=347 (Accessed 14 January 2022).

Sampson, R. (2015). 'Film Theory 101 - Laura Mulvey: The Male Gaze Theory', *Filminquiry.com*. Available at: https://www.filminquiry.com/film-theory-basics-laura-mulvey-male-gaze-theory/ (Accessed 19 January 2022).

'Second Wave Feminism: Collections' (2022). *Women's History Second Wave Feminism, Gale.com*. Available at: https://www.gale.com/primary-sources/womens-studies/collections/second-wave-feminism (Accessed 19 January 2022).

Shoemark, P. et al. (2020). 'Room to Glo: A systematic comparison of semantic change detection approaches with word embeddings'. *Association for Computational Linguistics*. doi: 10.18653/v1/D19-1007.

Spiro, M. (2001). 'Cultural Determinism, Cultural Relativism, and the Comparative Study of Psychopathology'. *Ethos,* 29(2), pp. 218-234. Available at: https://www.jstor.org/stable/640637 (Accessed 14 January 2022).

Sultana, A. (2012). 'Patriarchy and Women's Subordination: A Theoretical Analysis'. *Arts Faculty Journal*, 4. doi:10.3329/afj.v4i0.12929.

Tate (2022). 'Art Term: Young British Artists (YBAs)', *Tate.org*. Available at: https://www.tate.org.uk/art-terms/y/young-british-artists-ybas (Accessed 16 January 2022).

Walby, S. (1989). Theorising Patriarchy. *Sociology*, *23*(2), pp. 213–234. Available at: http://www.jstor.org/stable/42853921 (Accessed 14 January 2022).

White, P. (2022). 'ITV Orders UK Version Of Hit Reality Series "The Masked Singer"', *Deadline*. Available at: https://deadline.com/2019/05/itv-the-masked-singer-1202624853/ (Accessed 16 January 2022).

Willis, E. (1984). 'Radical Feminism and Feminist Radicalism.' *Social Text*, 9(10), pp. 91–118. https://doi.org/10.2307/466537.

Dana Leslie

Further Reading

The following texts were consulted as background research reading prior to embarking upon this dissertation. They are included here as a reading resource.

Bates, L. (2015). *Everyday Sexism*. London: Simon & Schuster.

Braderman, J et al. (1977) 'The First Issue Collective', *Heresies: A Feminist Publication on Art and Politics 1*, 1(1).

Butler, C. and Mark, L. (2007). *WACK! Art and the Feminist Revolution*. Los Angeles: Museum of Contemporary Art.

Carlson, M. (2004). *Performance: a critical introduction*. 2nd ed. London: Routledge.

Criado-Perez. (2019). *Invisible Women: Exposing data bias in a world designed for men*. London: Chatto & Windus.

Cwynar-Horta, J. (2016). 'The Commodification of the Body Positive Movement on Instagram', *Stream: Interdisciplinary Journal of Communication*, 8(2), pp.36–56. doi: 10.21810/strm.v8i2.203.

Daniels, M. et al. (2018). 'Beauty, Effort, and Misrepresentation: How Beauty Work Affects Judgments of Moral Character and Consumer

Preferences', *Journal of Consumer Research*, 45(1). pp. 126–147. doi:10.1093/jcr/ucx116.

Davis, S. et al. (2007). 'Effects of union type on division of household labour: Do cohabiting men really perform more housework?' *Journal of Family Issues*, 28(9), pp. 1246–1272. doi: 10.1177/0192513X07300968.

Dijkstra, S. (1980). 'Simone de Beauvoir and Betty Friedan: The Politics of Omission', *Feminist Studies,* 6(2), pp. 290-303, DOI: 10.2307/3177743.

Dobson, A. (2015). *Postfeminist Digital Cultures: Femininity, Social Media, and Self-Representation.* London: Palgrave Macmillan

Duffy, B. and Hund, E. (2015). '"Having it All" on Social Media: Entrepreneurial Femininity and Self-Branding Among Fashion Bloggers'. *Social Media and Society* (1). doi:10.1177/2056305115604337.

Elliott, A. (2001). *Concepts of the Self.* Cambridge: Polity Press.

Gill, R. (2003). 'From Sexual Objectification to Sexual Subjectification: The Resexualisation of Women's Bodies in the Media'. *Feminist Media Studies.* 3(1). pp. 100-106. doi.org/10.1080/1468077032000080158.

Harrison, K. and Martins, N. (2011). 'Racial and Gender Differences in the Relationship Between Children's Television Use and Self-Esteem: A Longitudinal Panel Study'. *Communication Research*, 39(3). doi: 10.1177/0093650211401376

Holland, J. et al. (2016) 'Trends in hospital admission rates for anorexia nervosa in Oxford (1968–2011) and England (1990–2011): Database studies', *Journal of the*

Royal Society of Medicine, 109(2), pp. 59–66. doi: 10.1177/0141076815617651.

Major, L. (2020). 'Love Island's Laura opens up about disaster boob jobs she deeply regrets', *The Sun*. Available at: https://www.thesun.co.uk/fabulous/12265825/laura-anderson-love-island-boob-job-regret/ (Accessed 4 January 2022).

McMillan, K. (2019). 'Representation of Female Artists in Britain During 2018'. *Freelands Foundation Research*. Available at: https://freelandsfoundation.imgix.net/documents/Representation-of-Female-Artists-in-Britain-Research-2018.pdf (Accessed 19 December).

Moi, T. (1999). *What is a woman? and other essays*. Oxford: Oxford University Press.

Molesworth, H. (2000). 'House Work and Art Work', 92 (October), pp. 71–97.

Montgomery, K.C. (2007.) *Generation Digital: Politics, commerce, and childhood in the age of the internet*. Cambridge, Mass: MIT Press.

Robinson, H. (2001). *Feminism Art Theory: An Anthology 1968-2000*. Oxford: Blackwell Publications.

Ryan, B. (2009). 'Manifesto for Maintenance: A Conversation with Mierle Laderman Ukeles'. *Art in America*. Available at: https://www.artinamericamagazine.com/newsfeatures/interviews/draft-mierle- interview/ (Accessed 12 December 2021).

Stewart, J. (2004). 'What Do Male Nonworkers Do?', *Bureau of Labour Statistics.* Available at: https://www.bls.gov/osmr/research-papers/2004/pdf/ec040010.pdf (Accessed 16 December 2021).

Woman and Equalities Committee (2020). 'Body Image Survey Results'. *Woman and Equalities Committee in the House of Commons.* Available at: https://publications.parliament.uk/pa/cm5801/cmselect/cmwomeq/805/80502.htm (Accessed 17 December).

Acknowledgements

Firstly, I would like to thank my mum and dad for always encouraging me to pursue art and doing all that they can to help me with my education. Secondly, I would like to thank Catriona and Sam, without whom I would never have made it this far.

Thank you to all the amazing artists that I not only get to research, but am fortunate enough to work alongside every day at DJCAD. I am grateful to Ellie Harrison for introducing me to Mierle Laderman Ukeles, and to my friend Ava, who not only asked if I knew of an artist called Lynn Hershman Leeson, but who has been beside me for every step of this degree to converse, collaborate and, most importantly, challenge me. I must also extend my thanks to all my wonderful colleagues and managers at my jobs; Discovery Point, DCA and the V&A Dundee, who gave me advice and listened with understanding when schedules clashed.

Lastly, I would like to express my sincere gratitude to my supervisor Helen Gorrill, who gave up her time to offer me guidance even before I was her student: her passion for teaching, writing and helping her students is inspiring and without her I would not have had the confidence to write this dissertation.

BOOM!

This book was originally submitted as a dissertation in partial fulfilment of the requirements of a Bachelor of Arts (Hons) degree in Fine Art at the Duncan of Jordanstone College of Art and Design, the University of Dundee, in 2022.

Dana Leslie

A note about Boom Graduates

We propel graduates forward so they can make their mark on the world - we push the boundaries, share brilliant ideas and inspire possibility. We publish dissertations as books, presented gift-boxed at graduation ceremonies, delivering brand-new research to the world quicker than anyone else. We plant trees for every commissioned book sold, and give our Boom graduates the chance to profit-share from their brilliant ideas. Furthermore we donate the majority of our profits to funding research and scholarship for disadvantaged students who wouldn't normally be able to attend university. Through academic excellence and environmental sustainability, *Boom Graduates* are changing the world.

We are Boom Graduates - an imprint of Boom Publications Ltd. We are a more-than-profit company, dedicating over half our profits to providing university scholarships for underprivileged students across the world. We aim to become the globe's biggest provider of such scholarships – and if like Dana, the author of this book, you'd also like to contribute to making the world a better place, please contact us: we publish monographs, edited books, and moreover our graduate series – Boom Graduates – are presented at graduation days across the world in archival, lined museum-quality presentation cases, engraved with the graduate's name and award.

Boom Publications are based at the Duncan of Jordanstone College of Art and Design, at the University of Dundee in Scotland. We were one of the winners of the 2022 Venture awards hosted by the Centre for Entrepreneurship, and have since been shortlisted for the Converge Challenge, a national award that brings together ambitious and creative thinkers with innovative ideas to work with industry experts to transform their ideas into sustainable companies operating in the commercial world. We are also climate conscious and work with agencies to plant a tree for each and every book commissioned, offsetting thousands of tonnes of carbon each year. Follow us on social media to watch our forest grow @boomgraduates.

Thank you for contributing by purchasing this book. Please visit our catalogues on www.boompublications.com.

Dana Leslie

Notes

Dana Leslie

Performing Feminism

Dana Leslie

Performing Feminism

Dana Leslie

Performing Feminism

www.ingramcontent.com/pod-product-compliance
Lightning Source LLC
Chambersburg PA
CBHW070232220526
45465CB00004B/1405